Mindfulness For Beginners:

Your Practical and Easy Guide to Be Peaceful, Relieve Stress, Anxiety and Depression Right Now!

Susan Mori

Table of Contents

INTRODUCTION:

Life is riddled with a seemingly never ending and unshakable misery. After solving one problem or accomplishing one task, you are off grappling with the next. Even vacations can't seem to alleviate the stress, because at the back of your head you are thinking how your money would have been better spent on investments because who knows what might happen in the future?

The problem with misery is that it breeds the self's worst possible enemy: the self. When the mind harbors worries, problems, and a sense of hopelessness, it cultivates unnecessary burdens such as stress, anxiety and depression. And if left unaddressed, this could deepen and crush the spirit of an unsuspecting individual.

The reason why you're looking at this book right

now is to help relieve yourself from these strong, negative feelings. You wish to know how to meditate and what benefits you can earn from it. Well, this book offers more than knowledge. Even if it's difficult, it tries to impart wisdom because being practical entails being purposeful.

This book holds an unconventional approach in guiding you through meditation. Most other book will tell you what to do and how to do it, but seldom will tell you why you should do it. There is the obvious answer of relieving oneself of stress, anxiety and depression, but the reader must understand that by practicing meditation, he opts to dig deeper. Hence, there is an expanded list of topics thoroughly discussed in this book.

Meditation is an internal process that begins by taming every human being's greatest source of power – the mind. Being an integral part of meditation, it is therefore important to include topics on how to understand how the mind works.

Although meditation according to known history

began years ahead of Buddhism, the principles of the latter shall be discussed to prepare the reader spiritually and mentally for the practice.

Of course, both the mental and physical benefits of meditation shall be enumerated. And to cap things off, this book lists some of the most frequently asked questions and their answers.

Chapter 1: Meditation Basics

What Meditation Actually Is and What it Isn't

When picturing how meditation is done, most people would imagine having to sit in lotus position while keeping his eyes closed and breathing "Ohm!" in a sort of trance. And when asked what goes on inside, it is a common conception that the mind is free or is being freed of any thought or emotion.

Such an image isn't particularly wrong, but it isn't the only method of meditation, either. There are more than one type of meditation technique, and one lets the person focus on a specific object.

Instead of keeping the mind blankly fixated on this thing or idea, the mind familiarizes itself with it. And in this book, this type of meditation shall be further discussed in the succeeding pages.

It may now thus occur to you that people actually meditate every day. When, for example, a person focuses on a certain object or matter, scrutinizes its advantages and disadvantages, and then enumerates the benefits he will reap from it, he practices meditation.

Illustration:

Buying a car requires weeks, or perhaps months, of contemplation. The process would commonly start with the establishment of the needs the buyer, and then followed by the determination of which car type will best serve this need. Afterwards, the buyer will research on the differences or advantages offered by each car brand. He could read reviews on the internet, prod friends with the same car type to reveal problems, or talk to car dealers about the best value for their money.

After gathering sufficient information, the buyer will now weigh the options in his mind. As he develops an inclination towards one, his desire to possess this specific brand and type of car deepens.

And as illustrated above, the essential exercise of contemplating which car to buy already results to meditation. Analytical processes may vary from person to person, but the same is true when selecting a university to enter, a house or apartment to live in, or more commonly, when selecting a person to marry. In fact, the very act of purchasing this book constitutes a part of meditation.

Because meditation can be exercised on any object, may it be concrete or abstract, it can also be done anywhere. It may be done while in the car, during a commute, while engaging in crafts, or while sitting alone on the sofa at home.

It is not necessary to find a darkened room or an airy garden to have to practice meditation. This book is all about practicality, hence the methods for meditation it shall discuss are those which will require no extra formal effort from the reader. It will instead focus on the substantial aspect of the practice.

Meditation as a Tool for the Perpetuation of Unvirtuous Thoughts

After having learned of the simplicity of meditation, a question now succeeds: "If I meditate every day, why am I still experiencing stress, anxiety or depression?"

This is because most people focus their mental efforts towards unvirtuous acts rather than virtuous ones.

Illustration:

When stuck in traffic, instead of focusing on the virtue of patience, the person is more likely to contemplate on the stupidity of the system, the incompetence of the traffic enforcers, the inconvenience from the construction happening on the street ahead, or the drivers who have caused the jam.

Many are not aware of its effect, but feeding this negative thought only strengthens the resolve and results only to greater stress. The simple idea that "the traffic enforcers are stupid" may evolve to, "they aren't doing their job properly", then to "my taxes are going to waste with these blokes". Feeding the thought further shall transform to anger. And should traffic persists, a circumstance outside the control of anyone stuck in it, anger can only ball up to stress and weigh down the spirits of the person.

Another example which every person may relate to better is thinking how much contempt they have over another. And in most cases, the subject of this contempt is one's boss.

This little seed of negativity will burrow deep in the crevices of the mind and shall be nurtured by every little observable fault the person does.

The emotion will find its way to the heart when it is shared with others. Hatred will bloom once, during his meditations, the person integrates his or her thoughts with what he or she learned from others.

These strong negative emotions are like poison inflicted upon one's self. It destroys no one but the person who harbors them. No one has died from anger or hatred, but these and others of the same kind invite stress, and later on, despair and depression. And when discussing these emotions with other people, instead of relieving oneself of the weight, he does the opposite.

It is easier to meditate upon all the bad things in life the same way it is easier to love junk food than vegetables. There are no explanations yet as to why, or if there is, it's not in this book, but you will discover later on that to cultivate peace through meditation, the mind undergoes the same process.

MORE THAN READING

Before discussing the actual practice of meditation, understand that by choosing and reading this book, you have already started.

Meditation is a mental exercise, but unlike those geared towards improving aptitude, knowing is not enough. Upon reading the texts of this book, you would have gained intelligence. Peace, and thus relief from stress, anxiety and depression, however, is developed through discipline.

To help you practice this mental discipline as early as now, exercises and their corresponding guidelines will be supplied throughout the book. You may choose to do them or not. But should you opt for the latter, this book implores that you subject its words under critical analysis. Do not take them as they are, and instead, ask yourself a thousand different why's.

> *Why are Buddhist principles discussed when I only need to know how to meditate?*

Why is this book so abstract when I was expecting it to be more concrete; like help me give an alternative to the lotus position?

Why are the roots of my depression being discussed when I only want relief?

Why does this book say I shouldn't settle in unvirtuous thoughts, but it at the same time encourages me to think about them?

Why is this book so long?

Why does it seem that concepts are being discussed repetitively?

Why should I even believe what this book is saying?

Why shouldn't I question the validity of everything it says?

Exercise 1:

What to do: Before moving to the next subchapter, take the time to think about the unvirtuous thoughts that you have entertained in the past. Below are some guide questions to help you identify what these are:

- Is there a person you hate, or is currently irritating you?
- Are there aspects of your job which you despise?
- Is there something about your special other that makes you want to break up with him or her?
- Are there things or matters within your family that encourage establishing and maintaining distance?
- Are there things about yourself you do not like?
- Is there anything in your daily life which you especially dislike, like the commute, the traffic, or the climate?

Important Note! If your answer to any of the above questions is in the affirmative, stop yourself from thinking any further. Like an open door that leads to a trap, the emotions associated with the objects asked about will pull you like gravity. And before you even know it, you will once again be snagged by and be drowning in unvirtuous thoughts.

Instead, however, stop before the door, refrain from crossing it, and calmly look at the view inside. *"Yes, there is a person I hate at the moment,"* and **stop!** Do not let the hateful thought—the very substance of this emotion—follow. But should it be inevitable, let it pass by as if you are watching a passing cloud, and then move on to the next door.

Objective: This exercise is like a precursor to meditation. It seeks to develop objectivity in the mind. Although it doesn't help you diminish emotions completely, which is absolutely impossible, it allows your mind to stay analytical without being influenced by feelings.

Chapter 2: Analytical Meditation

Focusing on a Single Object

Much like how the brain works when contemplating on the purchase of a car, the mind becomes critical in analytical meditation. And unlike in daily mental musings where the mind jumps from one thought to another, this method of meditation requires that all critical analysis be focused on one object only.

The object can be something that the senses can affect, like breathing. And it can also be an abstract concept such as patience.

Process: Begin the meditation by critically familiarizing yourself with the object. If, for example, the object is patience, you may start your analysis by contemplating on its benefits.

- ☐ How will patience affect a certain circumstance? Will it change according to your will? Or will it stay the same?
- ☐ If you remain patient on a given situation, like traffic, what thoughts would be running through your head instead?
- ☐ Does patience come with scientifically proven health benefits?

These questions do not need immediate answering if the answers haven't revealed themselves yet. Questioning, in fact, already constitutes critical analysis. What's important in this initial step is that you start the ball rolling.

Afterwards, try to expand your analysis beyond the benefits.

- ☐ Can patience be practiced only by silence? Or is there a way of practicing it whereby you express what's on your mind?
- ☐ Harboring patience can change or control a

person's mood. But is there a way of using patience to influence the behavior of people around?

Important Note! Keep in mind of the requisite of staying focused on the single object. By asking questions and trying to answer them, different ideas and thoughts will rise. And eventually, you may find yourself in the middle of chasing another object.

Thinking is easy. It's what the brain does from the moment you wake to the second you fall asleep. The difficult part in meditation is trying to stay focused on this single object. This is where discipline will be practiced.

Of course, in your meditations, the questions you've come up with must be answered. Researching for answers from books or online resources is alright. Answering the questions subjectively is fine as well. But as what this book has encouraged you to do, go beyond knowing. Be critical with everything you read or know.

Illustration:

In the first question, if the circumstance is being stuck in traffic, the obvious answer is that patience will change nothing. It will not clear the road for you; that is a fact. But go beyond this knowledge by thinking, "Hey! Neither does anger. Traffic is something I cannot control, after all." And then compare and weigh patience against anger. Think of how they would affect your mood, and how it will then affect your day, and how it will affect your behavior towards other people.

If, on the other hand, the circumstance is having to deal with a barista in Starbucks not working at your ideal pace, patience again will not change anything. And then it might occur to you that expressing exasperation will. Alerted by your loud indignant voice, and alarmed by the sight of your knitted eyebrows, the slow barista might just get the kick he needs to double time. You must expand, however, your musings to what's around you and the barista. Imagine how the people in Starbucks would react to the outburst. A group of girls might snicker in the corner while throwing meaningful glances at your direction. Other baristas might roll their eyes at the incident and make a mental note to avoid you in the future. And then imagine how you would feel if you catch any of these tiny and silent reactions.

And then think of how the scene might've changed if you instilled patience instead. The people in Starbucks would have continued with whatever they were doing and not realize your existence. The baristas would not have cared who you are. But you did, however, maintained the peace within you.

Goal: The goal in analytical meditation is to empathize or develop a certain closeness with the object, and then apply this new sense of familiarity of the object whenever apt.

Like researching on the benefits, specs and reviews of a certain car, the more you know, the more you feel captivated by it. At some point even, you will feel personally attached to it. And when, for example, you are faced by an adverse opinion of it, because you know every single detail of the car, you may rebut the claim with a well-constructed and logical counter-statements. You might also react to the adversity by agreeing to it because you recognize and accept its flaws.

Illustration:

Following the example in the previous topic, which is patience, the goal is to not simply know the answers to the questions you have initially set forth. You must also aim to combine positive emotions with the object, and then apply them whenever necessary.

Going back to the Starbucks example, say you are stuck between staying patient and bursting into anger. If you choose to stay patient—to not say a word—but cannot control the raging fire inside, then your meditation has not helped you reach your objective. Your inner peace was still disturbed because you only know that patience is a virtue, and that it is the right choice. However, this virtue has not yet been instilled as yours, which is why the negative emotion remained.

If, however, during your meditations you were able to fully empathize with patience; that you were able to develop a closeness to it that it seems you are the embodiment of patience itself, then you wouldn't even reach that point where you have to choose between staying patient and bursting into anger.

Objective: What good will come out of this method of overthinking? You get to discover the truth on your own. And when the truth has bloomed from your heart and mind on its own, no one will be able to take it away from you, hence the critical analysis.

Illustration:

It is similar with introducing religion to a person. A child will believe God exists if told. However, upon reaching adulthood, this belief would also have been easy to take away given enough knowledge to believe otherwise.

A critical person, before completely throwing his beliefs through the window, would first question. *Is God real?* Similar with what has been discussed in this book, the person will undergo meditation. He will seek the truth through critical analysis.

This is a personal journey. Although

mentors and books such as this one may guide the person, everything will still be subjected under his scrutiny. Once however the journey is complete, the truth will naturally bloom from the heart.

Later on, whenever faced with adverse evidence or knowledge, his belief and his peace will not be disturbed because he knows in his heart what is true.

Important Note! Because in analytical meditation the person remains critical in his familiarization with the object, he has the option to choose one of the subjects incited in Exercise 1.

Instead, however, of looking outward and at the person, practice inward reflection. Drop the habit of finding more reasons to feel contempt. Instead, try to understand why you feel that way. Ask yourself why you think his actions annoy you when others, despite having the same faults, do not.

If your contempt is great, and the emotions

associated with it rise, take control of it by applying what you have learned in Exercise 1. And then continue with your meditation.

Where and When to Practice: As previously discussed, meditation can be done anywhere and at any time. It can even be done concurrently with other activities. However, for the purposes of this book, you are encouraged to dedicate a specific time of the day for the practice.

If you live on your own, the perfect times would be in the morning immediately after waking up, and in the evening right before sleeping. And you may meditate on your bed if you can manage to stay awake for 15 minutes. If not, then choose any part of your home where you can focus and hear nothing but your thoughts.

If, on the other hand, you live with others, or if there are kids in the house, find a 15-minute period on your daily schedule where you are sure you will not be bothered. Then if a quiet and private room would be impossible to find, try looking for peaceful spots in a nearby park. If that's impossible as well, go for an uncrowded coffee shop.

When meditating in a public place, drown the buzz of the crowd by listening to instrumental music. You run the risk of being mistaken for a felon if you sit in a corner intently staring at blank space, so bring a cup of drink with you to look less suspicious.

Important Notes!

- ☐ **15-minute period**: Initially, meditating for 5 to 6 minutes a day would be sufficient. The reason why you need to dedicate a longer time, however, is because getting into the meditative state requires more time.

  The meditative state is achieved when you are able to push the noises in your head aside. And when you are ready to bring your selected object to the centerstage of your conscious-ness.

It may sound easy, but in reality, you will grapple with the urge to check your phone for new emails, or with the thought that this little time would be better dedicated to dealing with deadlines. And this is why the morning (immediately after waking up) is the most ideal time for meditation. Before the wave of errands comes crashing on your consciousness, you have already and successfully meditated.

- **Peace and quiet:** Even in the middle of the most crowded train or in the noisiest streets, people sometimes slip into a meditative state effortlessly. For this practice, however, the ideal environment is somewhere peaceful and quiet. This is because meditation requires immense discipline from you.

When you focus on an object, your brain gets too tired or bored that it starts chasing other thoughts. And unfortunately, a stimulus-rich environment offers the best distractions. One moment you could be at the brink of uncovering the root of patience, but then you saw a baby on a stroller and you suddenly remembered you have to buy diapers so you have to not forget to stop by at Costco after work, and taking advantage of the visit, you might as well buy eggs, bread, and coffee for breakfast tomorrow, which then reminds you of the laundry which needs pressing because you and the kids would have nothing to wear tomorrow.

Most importantly, because discipline is often associated with punishment, treat meditation as a form of relaxation. Look at it as that time of the day where you get to drop all worries on the ground; that very special 5 minutes you spend exclusively for your personal growth and well-being.

Exercise 2:

What to do: You will now fully engage in meditation. Opting for an object of your own choosing is ideal because no one knows best what beautiful truth should bloom in your heart. If you find the object challenging to meditate on, however, a less complex subject might be more beneficial. Below are some subjectively easy objects, and their corresponding guide questions to help you jumpstart the practice:

- *Romantic Love*
- How do you know when you're in love? How do you distinguish the feeling from mere infatuation or lust?
- Can man live without romantic love? And can his life be well lived even in its absence?
- What is the root of romantic love? Is it inside the person who loves? Or is it the person he or she loves? Will love then be extinguished by the passing of the person being loved?

- Can there only be one romantic love in a lifetime? Or is it possible to truly love more than one person? Is an "ultimate" love real?

- *Sorrow*

- Why is it difficult to convert this emotion to acceptance? Is it even possible to convert it to acceptance?

- Can sorrow be alleviated by something other than time?

- How do you get by this powerful emotion? Do you drown yourself in alcohol? Do you lock yourself up in a darkened room? Do you talk to people about it?

- If a person's happiness over something be greater, does that mean that the loss of this something stirs greater sorrow in return?

- *Death*

- What is your relationship with death? Is it a friend, a foe, or a mere stranger?

- Is it possible to feel grief and joy concurrently in the passing of a loved one?

- What will life be without death? Would life even

33

be worth living without it?

- ☐ Is there a correlation between death and overpopulation? If there is, does this mean the world is out of balance?

- ☐ *War*

- ☐ What is the purpose of war? Why do some men despise it, while others yearn for it?

- ☐ Can there be war without death and damage?

- ☐ Will humans even realize peace without having to go through war?

- ☐ In the past, wars were started primarily to conquer territories. How have wars evolved from then? What do people fight for in modern wars?

Duration: Stick to this exercise for a week or two. For your first try, limit your meditation to 3 minutes. See how many times you've caught yourself drifting to unfocused thoughts. When you feel that you've already improved, increase the time by one minute.

Important   Note!

Prepare an alarm so you wouldn't have to anxiously glance at the clock during meditation. Make sure, however, to set the volume low and to select a less distressing tone. The mind needs to ease slowly out of meditation.

Remember, in preparing to enter the meditative state, you unload your worries one by one. It makes sense, therefore, that in leaving such a peaceful state, you load back your worries in the same manner. If your alarm creates distress in your mind, it will feel like the fire alarm broke out while you were enjoying a nice hot shower, and without thinking, you load the fridge on your back and run through the door while still naked.

Objective: Like how a novice pianist familiarizes himself with the keys, the objective of this exercise is to help you get to know your mind a little better. You will learn that your concentration has limits and that your mind is a difficult stallion to tame.

Chapter 3: Zazen

Introduction to Formal Meditation

The meditation technique discussed in the previous chapter is purely substantive. It focuses on how the mind should regulate thoughts, and how it should focus on an object. As to how the body should be positioned during meditation—whether sitting down, standing up, leaning against a wall, or reclining on the bed, none was provided. The only inkling of form in analytical meditation is the time that is encouraged to be dedicated in a day. But even that isn't absolute; they are mere recommendation which you can opt to disregard.

Formal meditation, on the other hand, requires religious dedication and a sacred space to be practiced—pretty much like how most prayers are done. It often comes hand-in-hand with a set of principles and virtues the person is enjoined to embody, such as the case with Buddhism. And depending on the type of formal meditation, it often seeks to discipline both the mind and the body.

Between formal and informal meditation, the latter is more practical because it's easier to fit in any schedule. This makes it ideal for those with barely any time left for himself in a day. And because informal meditation is not too selective of location, it can be done in the most convenient of places, even in the bathroom.

If, however, you wish to improve your posture and your breathing, which also contributes in relieving stress, anxiety and depression, then opt for formal meditation.

Also, if in case you find informal meditation

difficult to practice because of lack of structure, the opposite might be more suitable for you. The formal meditation which shall be discussed in this book is, in fact, a lot simpler to perform because no critical analysis is required. It is less taxing and more relaxing.

ZAZEN

There is more than one type of formal meditation and each is associated with a specific discipline such as mindfulness and openness. Others go as far as focusing on the energies of the body and directing them to the heart, the core or wherever. But because this book serves as a practical guide to meditation, it shall focus on the most practical of them all: Zazen.

Zazen is the method of meditation practiced by Zen Buddhists. Among the several types of meditation, this form greatly appeals to beginners because the concept is easy to understand, and the form is versatile enough to allow individuals with physical problems and difficulties to practice zen meditation. Also, because Zazen doesn't require practitioners to study a set of principles rooted in Buddhism, it can be practiced in conjunction with any type of religion.

Mental Discipline in Zazen

Interestingly, the difference between analytical meditation and Zazen isn't too wide. You also have to familiarize yourself with an object in the latter. Unlike in analytical meditation, however, where you can choose different objects in every session, the only object in Zazen is your breathing.

During Zen meditation, the practitioner sits and counts his breath. It's as easy as that; no critical analysis is needed. Of course, however, every discipline comes with a challenge, and in Zazen, it's living in the present.

According to Zen Buddhism, most people are trapped in either the past or the future. Those who settle in the past often feel depressed, thinking of what they could and should have changed to set the present right. Those who live in the future, on the other hand, are often visited by anxiety because they constantly think of what might and should be. In this very demanding world where expectations are constantly set and setting expectations has become a way of life; where people are trapped in a cycle of never ending tasks, moving onward to the next after finishing one, people actually forget to live in the present. They forget to take a break, and just appreciate the moment.

The idea behind Zazen, therefore, is to discipline the mind to set worries aside and simply be in the present.

Of course, because you'll be sitting the entire time in a quiet room, nothing exciting would be going on while "living the present." The discipline you apply during meditation, however, will eventually and naturally become a state of mind. You will learn to live the present even outside of meditation.

Perhaps, on your next trip to the tropics, instead of planning on what Instagram-worthy pics to take because you need a hundred likes and a dozen more followers, you will actually enjoy the sun, sand and sea. Instead of worrying that people will think you're cheap and ugly because you didn't post photos of you on a fancy boat looking pretty and sexy, feel the wind and the spray of the ocean on your face as you ride that boat.

Process: After assuming the proper posture, which shall be discussed in detail later, the practitioner regulates his breathing. There is no need to stick to a count even when there is a recommended rhythm. Simply inhale deep and exhale as you naturally do, keeping a regular rhythm. Being too technical with breathing will only take your concentration away from the substantial aspect of the practice.

Afterwards, pour your focus on counting your breath. Once you reach ten counts, repeat back to one.

A common misconception in Zen meditation is that you empty your mind. That, of course, is impossible because as long as the mind is awake, thoughts will come and go. In actuality, Zen meditation redirects your thoughts to your breathing. Once you are able to achieve this strenuous task, instead of reliving that horrible breakup in your head, you would hear the beat of your heart, the sound of air passing through your nostrils, and even the rush of blood through your veins. This is what it means to live in the moment.

All this may sound easy, but it actually isn't because as described earlier, the mind is a difficult stallion to tame. When left alone with no one but yourself, with nothing but the wall, and doing nothing but sit, the thoughts in your head starts talking louder and clearer. And the issue here is that you wouldn't even know you have been listening to them the entire practice. You will only notice that your consciousness has been drifting when you've already lost count of your breath, or when emotions start stirring in your heart.

Thought, of course, cannot be pushed aside or blocked. And when you try to fight your thoughts, the stronger they become. So what you should do when they rise is to let them pass. Watch them as if you're passing by the window of an appliance store, glancing at the videos being played on the TV displays. When it's over, calmly resume your count, and feel the rise and fall of your chest.

One danger brought by passing thoughts, however, is getting triggered by the emotion they are associated with. The sole image of an empty bed could, for example, remind you of a failed relationship. And this could unleash a waterfall of emotions including reactions to the entire experience which is either regret or loathing. Unfortunately, some people unconsciously grip and cling to these emotions.

There are two ways to deal with these emotions during Zen meditation.

> *First*, similar with analytical meditation, you empathize. Upon the rise of these negative feelings, follow it up immediately with positive ones. Embrace them and realize that they are part of you now. You cannot, after all, extinguish the feeling the same way you cannot erase the memory.

After accepting the emotion, let them go as you exhale, then resume your count. Or if you've already lost count, start back at one.

Second, you watch these thoughts without judgement. Most Zen practitioners are able to maintain tranquility regardless of the thought that passes. And their secret in reaching this level of calmness is detachment.

Which of the two methods is more difficult is up to you to determine. Each person, after all, undergoes a unique meditation experience, and not everyone reacts the same to the rise of unwanted thoughts.

Objective:

Goal: In most formal meditations, the ultimate goal is to reach enlightenment. The same is true for Zazen. But because you're engaging in the practice to simply relieve stress, ease anxieties and fight of depression, your goal is to learn to perpetuate the state of tranquility.

Being tranquil means being calm not only during times of peace, but also during times of chaos.

A person undergoes massive stress when, for example, he's on his way to that long-awaited job interview. This interview is so important that it will actually determine the

Materials Needed

Zazen requires that you maintain a very specific posture throughout the practice. And this posture requires two specific materials to be achieved. Hence, before starting your practice, make sure you already have these items on hand.

Zafu and Zabuton: The Zafu is a small round cushion made specifically for Zen meditation, and the Zabuton is a rectangular cushion placed under the Zafu. These two are inseparable the same way a mortar never comes without a pestle.

https://www.amazon.com/Buckwheat-Zafu-Zabuton-Meditation-Cushion/dp/B0046UHHNI

In assuming the lotus position, by sitting on the Zafu, your back is kept straight and strong allowing you to breathe better. Then because your knees will support the majority of your legs' weight, the Zabuton is purposely placed under to keep them comfortable.

This pair isn't difficult to find. They are available in a multitude of online stores, and they also come in different colors and designs. If, however, you don't want to shed money out for a Zafu and Zabuton, you can always of for make-do options.

The perfect substitute for a Zafu is an ordinary

cushion or pillow that isn't too wide, but is thick enough to raise you significantly from the floor. The dimensions of a Zafu is 14 inches in diameter and 8 inches in height; finding a substitute close to that measure will greatly benefit the practice.

The Zabuton, on the other hand, can be substituted by seat cushions. However, you must find one that is wide enough to fit your crossed legs. The regular size of a Zabuton is 30 by 28 inches. If a wide, flat cushion isn't your ordinary household item, you may opt for folded comforters instead. The only problem with this option, however, is that comforters might be too fluffy that when you place the make-do Zafu and sit, your weight will press down on this end and leave the knees on almost the same level with your buttocks.

Clothes

In Zen, even the clothes you wear matter. Because you'll be sitting in a relatively complicated position, you need clothes that do not restrain. Otherwise, instead of focusing on your breathing, you'll be stuck thinking how cramped your legs are, or how much pain your crotch is in.

The traditional clothing worn by Japanese Zen Buddhists is called Samue – a pair of kimono-style jacket and trousers that comes in solid, muted colors.

https://www.seidoshop.com/products/deluxe-cotton-samue

There's no need to invest on this specific type of clothing, but you do need to wear clothes that are loose enough to keep your body comfortable. Even wearing socks during Zen meditation isn't recommended. Pajamas and robes as substitutes will do.

Other things to note in choosing clothing for Zen meditation is color and pattern. Loud prints and bright colors are discouraged because it distracts the mind. Thus, sticking to muted, earthy colors is highly preferred. Just for additional information, Samue don't often come in white.

If, however, you are planning to practice on your own, you can afford to be a little lax on the color of your clothes. Zen is often practiced in a group headed by a master. And the reason why there is a preference for muted colors is so that others won't get distracted. Unless you meditate in front of a mirror, you don't normally see your own clothes save for your trousers. You therefore won't be distracting anybody should you go for a black shirt with a large sunflower print at the center.

Form and Posture

Breathing: Breathe through your nose naturally and quietly. When exhaling, use your abdomen to expel all the air from your lungs. If you can't take long deep breaths, take short ones. What's important here is that you breathe in a steady rhythm.

Posture: Zazen is keen on form. To expound on this point, it has provided specific postures for the legs, back, neck, hands and even the mouth and the eyes. Although it didn't originate from Japan, it was cultivated and perpetuated by the Japanese, hence the attention to details. Know, however, that each minute requirement, such as keeping the eyes cast downward at 45 degrees, is backed with purpose. Following each like how one measures the ingredients of a delectable chocolate cake is therefore necessary.

Legs – The most popular position among Zen practitioners is the Lotus Position because it offers the best stability. However,

51

if your body isn't flexible enough, or that this position is simply too complex, you may opt for the other options provided below:

- ☐ <u>Full Lotus</u> - Both feet rests over their opposite thighs in this position, keeping the body symmetrical and stable.

https://www.123rf.com/photo_76735714_woman-doing-yoga-meditating-in-full-lotus-pose-with-hands-in-namaste-in-studio.html

- Half Lotus - The left foot is placed over the right thigh while the other is comfortably tucked under. Although this position is generally more convenient than the full lotus, it keeps the body asymmetrical. And because the back compensates to keep your body straight, you might develop back problems after continued practice. The solution here is to alternate your legs every meditation session.

https://www.youtube.com/watch?v=yTY12Qnff9w

▢ <u>Burmese</u> - Among the all the listed cross-legged positions in this book, the Burmese is the easiest to do and maintain. First, you sit on the front tip of the Zafu, then cross your legs on the Zabuton. The top of your feet, as well as your knees, should rest flatly on the rectangular cushion.

https://dandanyoga.com/2015/04/10/a-beginners-guide-to-meditation-what-i-learned-while-living-in-a-monastery/

▢ <u>Seiza</u> - In this position, the practitioner kneels the Japanese way: they sit on their upturned feet.

Seiza

The three most common problems people encounter, however, with this position are:

1) that their legs cannot bend all the way down disabling their buttocks to reach and rest on their feet;

2) that spending just a minute in this position already results in painful cramps, and;

3) that the weight of their upper body is too much for their ankles to carry.

There are two solutions to these problems. The first involves using the Zafu or pillow instead of your feet as cushion. You sit on it, but you keep your legs in a kneeling position, the calves and ankles embracing the Zafu.

Your second option is using a Seiza bench in place of a Zafu. As the name denotes, it is a kind of wooden chair specifically used for the Seiza position. The beauty of using this meditation accessory is that it takes all the weight off your ankles and keeps your spine straight.

http://www.michiganbuddhist.com/seiza/

▢ Chair - Finally, for those who cannot engage in any of the positions mentioned above, there's always the chair position. Here, you will literally use a chair for meditation. You will still need, however, the Zafu and Zabuton. Place the chair on the Zabuton, then sit on the front third of the chair, leaving ample space between your back and the backrest. Having your back rest on the chair will cause the spine to curve, thus making it difficult to perform the breathing exercise, hence the importance of this little space. If it's difficult for you to support and straighten your spine, use a Zafu as cushion for your back. If the chair is too high that your feet cannot lay flatly on the floor, use another pillow or Zafu as elevation.

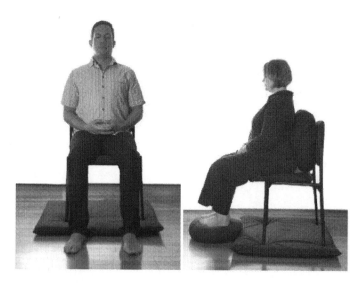

http://www.zen.org.nz/learn-how-to-meditate.html

If you do not exercise regularly, you might need to stretch before engaging in the more complex meditation positions. Stretching pulls the fibers of the muscles, causing them to realign and reorganize. This thus results in releasing the tightness of the muscles, making them more flexible and capable of performing a wider range of motions. In meditation, this preparatory exercise will allow you to sit comfortably in any of the above positions, and not have you struggle to bend your legs or to keep your legs bent.

Upper Body – As you may have already gleaned from the previous topic, a straight upper body is key in meditation. Do not mistake this, however, for the military style of erecting your spine. There's no need to strain your back as if some invisible force is pulling you from the head. Relax and do what comes naturally. The important thing here is you do not slouch.

If the legs need stretching, the waist and hips could use a healthy bending, too. And Zazen has a special way of doing this. Already in any of the sitting positions above, place your hands palm-up on your knees. Then like a bamboo dancing with the wind, without moving the hips, sway the torso. Lean from side to side, forward and back, like a pole starting with big movements and then gradually decreasing until you stop back at the center.

Neck and Head – The neck should follow the alignment of the spine. Pull your chin just enough to keep your crown high and reaching for the sky. Again, do not force your form; do what is natural for you while maintaining your posture.

Hands and Shoulders – Place your left hand palms-up over your right foot if you're in the Full Lotus position, or on your lap you're in the Saizen, Burmese, or Chair position.

Then, place the right hand, palms-up as well, over the left hand. Connect your two thumbs to create an oval. This hand position is called Cosmic Mudra or Hokkaijoin, and its purpose is to:

1) Bring the mind beyond duality by harmonizing its complex conditions, and;

2) Help the wandering mind realize that it is out of focus. The oval of your hand won't maintain its shape if the mind isn't on meditation.

http://www.zenbrighton.co.uk/hands/1

Your hands must be at the level of your navel, and the wrists must rest over your thighs. Relax your shoulders and let the arms fall naturally.

Mouth – In Zazen, even the tongue must adhere to form. Press it lightly on the roof of your mouth after swallowing once. The seal this will create will reduce salivation and thus reduce the need to swallow every now and then during meditation.

As mentioned before, all breathing should be done through the nose. Therefore, keep your mouth closed and your teeth clenched.

Eyes – The eyes remain open throughout the practice but are focused on nothing in particular. Keep your eyelids half-closed, and your eyes cast downwards at a 45-degree angle. This lessens the need to blink and prevents the practitioner from slipping into sleep or daydreaming.

Ideally, especially when meditating with friends, you should face wall. This prevents external movements from distracting your focus.

The posture requirements for Zazen are extensive, and for most people, unnatural. And you might spend your first sessions minding each part of your body instead of counting your breaths. The goal of Zen meditation is to mute the worries that constantly nag at a busy mind. These worries remain muted when accounting for each body part. So if you catch yourself minding your posture and losing count, don't hurry back to meditation. Correct what you find to be out of place and gently start back at one.

Where to Practice Zazen

The place of meditation is equally important as the posture. You can thus expect the same level of meticulousness in finding the right room for the practice. Before proceeding with the details, know that you can always opt for classes. It is possible that a Zen master resides in your area and organizes classes. These classes are often held in peaceful establishments surrounded by nature.

Although Zazen can be done individually and personally, having a master to mentor you is priceless. Not only will they correct your posture, they will guide you through the practice—how you can maintain your focus, what your state of mind should be, and if you're encountering problems, how to best overcome this. There would also be no need to invest on a Zafu and Zabuton, and possibly, on a Samue, and no need to look for a very specific space that will fit the requirements of the practice.

More importantly, in opting for classes, you get to join a community. It gives you the opportunity to meet people outside of your usual circles. Talking to them after class can open a fresh new perspective, giving analytical meditations (should you choose to practice this concurrently with Zazen) better foundations.

If, however, this isn't an option, going solo isn't so bad also.

Look for a room or a space with the following characteristics:

- *Enough light to keep the mind awake, but not too bright to cause pain in your eyes.* If you plan to find a spot outside the four corners of your house, like a garden, look for one under the shade of trees.
- *Temperature just right for you.* It must not be too hot to cause you to sweat, and not too cold to cause you to chill. Otherwise, your mind will focus on the discomfort, and how nice it would be if you had a jacket around. Air-conditioned rooms are alright, but consider the droning they make. The sound might distract you.
- *Silence or quiet.* The most important characteristic of a Zazen room is that it is peaceful. There is nothing that could bother your meditation such as rowdy neighbors, buzzing television screens, roaring traffic,

alarming phone calls, or disorderly children and pets. In the suburbs, a tree-lined backyard would be perfect. If you're in the city, however, a home office could be the closest possibility.

- *Muted colors or plain walls.* Traditional Zazen practitioners meditate facing the walls, and like the clothes they wear, they prefer its color to be plain and solid. Same with the purpose of almost every other detail discussed in this chapter, this is to give the mind no distractions during the practice. If you've decided to meditate in a room in your house, therefore, you might have to take down some of the decors and memorabilia hanged on the walls.

If in case you're aiming for garden meditation, the sight of nature, despite its beautiful mess, is alright. You can always opt to face the fence or direct your eyes on plain grass if you find yourself distracted by the garden's overwhelming details.

Final Pointers in Zazen

☐ Unlike in analytical meditation where you are free to change times or skip days, Zazen religiously follows a schedule—at least, preferably. Zen meditation is not only discipline for the mind and the body, but also of conduct. Similar with aiming to lead a healthier and more productive life, an individual not only changes his diet and his outlook, he also sticks to healthy habits like waking up at four in the morning or exercising for at least one hour everyday.

☐ Most solo practitioners dedicate a specific room or spot for the practice, and do not select places which are convenient at the moment. Think of it as something similar to an altar – a place where followers of a certain faith present themselves to offer prayers. Having this sacred spot somehow conditions the mind to enter into a meditative state whenever within it.

☐ Similar   with

analytical meditation, practitioners should ease into zen meditation by sitting down and assuming the proper posture without hurry. In the same manner, a practitioner should emerge from the practice slowly by allowing the blood to pump back into his still body.

Start with the hands. Lift them up from hokkaijoin by placing them palms-up on your thighs. For the torso, do the swaying exercise. Then for the legs, unfold and stretch one leg and then the other, and then let the blood flow back through them before standing up.

ZAZEN EXERCISES

Exercise 3

The mental discipline in Zazen is a lot simpler than in analytical meditation. Exercise 3, therefore, will be about actual physical exercises to help release the mind from the constraints of the body while undergoing Zen meditation.

There is another type of formal meditation called Qi Gong, and here, the practitioner engages the body in yoga-like movements while also undergoing meditation and breathing exercises. This was a better type of meditation to discuss because involving the body in meditation would better relieve stress, anxiety and depression. However, since not all people have the same level of physical capacity, Zazen was preferred. Apart from being simpler, it has provided posture options to make it adapt to the varying physical capacities of beginners.

Because, however, the movements in Qi Gong are

undeniably beneficial, this book will outline a few important exercises. These are all aimed at improving breathing and making the body more flexible—perfect preparatory exercises for Zazen.

1. *Warm-up*. Start by stepping your left foot out at shoulder width. Then, open your palms out and inhale through the nose as you raise your arms over your head. Turn your palms over then exhale through your mouth as you bring your arms back down. Sink your knees a little every time you breathe out and straighten them back when you raise your arms back up. Repeat at least 6 times.

2. *Painting with Light.* Assume the same stance as above. Slowly lift your arms forward up to shoulder height; your wrists relaxed. Then, in the same speed, let your arms fall as you exhale; your hands now opened forward. Again, bend your knees a little as you bring down your arm. Breathe in as you repeat by lifting

your arms back up, relaxing the wrists once more, and straightening the knees. The arm movement in this exercise is reminiscent of a paint brush.

3. *Opening the Energy Gates.* With your legs still shoulder width apart, face your palms towards each other, your arms lifted to shoulder height. Then inhale deep as you open your arms to its full extent as if opening the gates. Exhale as you close back the arms; your knees, again, bending slightly. Then repeat the movement by opening the arms once again. After performing this move at least 3 times, finish by bringing your hands to your chest, then bringing them down slowly as you exhale.

4. *Connecting Heaven and Earth.* Start this move by facing your palms at each other at your chest. Then, exhale as you calmly push your left arm upward and your right arm downward, stretching the back as a result. Inhale as you pull your arms back together,

letting the palms pass each other by your chest. Breathe out once more as you push your arms upward and downward, this time in vice versa. Repeat this movement 3 times, then finish by again bringing your hands to your chest, then pushing both hands slowly down.

Chapter 4: Settled Meditation

As a Conclusion to Analytical Meditation

This meditation technique shall be only discussed briefly, for unlike the previous two, the mind will not have to undergo critical analysis, and the body will not have to assume a specific posture.

Settled meditation only needs you to focus on an object like you do in analytical meditation, and familiarize yourself on it not through extensive reasoning, but by harboring positive emotion towards this object.

Illustration:

This practice is similar to the way an individual looks at his special other. There is no need to further know things about her nor understand why they are so. Or if there should be new things about her, it can only bring surprise and further wonder; being critically analytical about it wouldn't be the first to occur in his mind. The man only needs to think of her and feel the love he feels for her.

When in a long-distance relationship, for example, a man could have the opportunity to meet the most interesting woman in the country he's in. The circumstances could conspire to make it logical to take the chance and spend intimate days and nights with this woman. But if he had spent days savoring the feeling the love he has for his special other, he will never have to think twice on whether to act on this opportunity or not. He only needs to picture her face in his mind and the feeling of love is revived. Why else would he need such shallow and temporary relations? No amount of unsupported logic could trump this truth in his heart.

Settled meditation should be done after finding the truth through analytical meditation. As mentioned before, the truth could hurt you because it's not always what you expect. Whatever it is, however, it must lead you to a wider understanding, and thus compassion. This is where settled meditation should thus come in.

Focusing on the object and engulfing it with strong positive emotions during meditation will cause the feeling to become automatic.

Illustration:

Going back to the example of harboring contempt over a person, it is possible that through analytical meditation you discover that this strong negative emotion is actually caused by your own insecurities. It is not the person, therefore, who is faulty but you, and this truth would naturally hurt you.

What becomes then of the object person? More importantly, what becomes of the feeling of contempt? There are people who, despite knowing the truth, continue harboring the same negative emotions. These, after all, root from the heart, and everything that blooms from it cannot be easily removed. Hence the necessity for settled meditation.

When engaging in settled meditation with the same person as your object, you replace contempt with an equally strong emotion such as love and compassion. Of course, this process may take a while to take effect, because when you encounter the same person outside of meditation after your first few session, old feelings could still rise. This same natural reaction, however, also makes the best unit of measure in determining the effectivity of your meditation. You will know you have successfully replaced unvirtuous thoughts with virtuous ones when your natural reaction towards this person has become kindness.

SETTLED MEDITATION AS NOT THE FINAL PRACTICE

Nothing in this world is permanent, and the same is true with the feeling of compassion. There will be times when you feel this positive emotion weakening.

When this happens, understand that it's not you being weak. It could in fact be caused by a variety of reasons. Perhaps it's the layering of unfortunate events, thus giving you the feeling of vulnerability. And it's also possible that it's merely caused by physiological processes like hormonal imbalance. Of course, the reason could be more complex than that, but know that even those who has been practicing meditation for years remains susceptible to this feeling of weakness.

Its occurrence, therefore, makes it necessary that you go back to practice analytical meditation and not force these positive emotions through settled meditation.

Illustration

Continuing the example on long distance relationships, contrary to what was said earlier, even knowing he loves someone back at home, a man could find himself succumbing to the desire of being with another. This situation is in fact more resonant with reality. It is difficult to recall the feeling of genuine love towards his woman at home if all logic is against it.

Imagine now how difficult it would be to fight temptation by simply picturing the woman in your head and forcing the feeling of love on her. That to achieve this, the man recalls all the good times he spent with her, and how it made him feel. Instead of actually harboring love, it could backfire and leave you feeling tired instead. This, in fact, might just be the very reason why most relationships, whether be it in long distance or not, fail.

Think now how the man's outlook would be if, instead of forcing the feeling, he rationalizes why he loves her. And instead of recalling the good times, he recalls the reason why he stayed by her side during times of hardship. By undergoing this process, the man is once again reminded of the truth. And only when he finds the truth could he once again engage in savoring the fruit of this truth which is love.

The Grand Effect of Meditation

It may now thus have occurred to you that meditation expands your horizons; it opens the mind to countless epiphanies. And as a result, your heart opens to understanding. Understanding, in turn, leaves the mind at peace because it does not have to wonder and worry why things happened that way. And finally, when the mind is at peace, the body is freed from the grip of stress.

Although meditation relieves anxiety and depression altogether, if the roots of these two remain buried in the heart of a person, no matter how fast one cuts the fruits, they will inevitably grow back.

Much like physical fitness, meditation is not a temporary solution in relieving oneself of the burdens of the mind and the heart, but a discipline and a way of life. One of the primary goals of the practice to open the person's mind to a fresh perspective, and this cannot be achieved without separating oneself from old habits.

In analogy, a person wishing lose excess weight may do so with the help of diet programs – quick fixes that can deliver the desired results within months. Success is inevitable through such methods. However, the person will gain whatever he lost and possibly more once he stops the program and returns to his old lifestyle which may perhaps be excessive and unhealthy eating, smoking or abusive drinking—the root cause of his excess weight to start. It is therefore necessary for the person to separate himself from his old habits if he wishes to rid of his excess weight completely.

In meditation, the excess weight is the person's anxiety and depression, and the unhealthy lifestyle is his unreflected ways. The diet program is meditation, and to relieve the person completely of his excess baggage or prevent them from recurring, Buddhist principles shall be briefly discussed in the succeeding chapter.

CHAPTER 5: UNDERSTANDING THE SOURCE OF STRESS, ANXIETY AND DEPRESSION

NOISES

Noise, perhaps, is the source of all the negativity one experiences in life. And in this book, noise pertains to not only of aural noises, but also of visual noises and thought noises.

Aural noises are those that can be heard with the ears – the shriek of a baby, the horn of a passing train, the buzz of a busy crowd, or the murmur of the television. In contrast, visual noises are the colorful billboards, flashy advertisements and intriguing clickbaits. Thought noises, on the other hand, are internal; these are the unnecessary impressions that run through the mind.

Although one may be of the opinion that thought noises play a greater role in bringing stress, anxiety and depression, all actually conspires to take over your mind. Therefore, even if in the previous chapters thought noises are channeled and released, as long as visual and aural noises affect a person, these thoughts will never cease to stop.

Not everyone is aware of this fact, but this highly commercialized world is designed to manipulate every move a person makes. From choosing what food to eat and what clothes to wear, to what age to marry and which university to enter the kids, every person is somehow given benchmarks on what to attain in life.

Illustration:

By looking at the cover of a women's magazine with an image of a tall, slim, pretty, and young-looking middle-aged blonde celebrity in a revealing bikini standing in front of the words "Secrets to Staying Young" and "Workouts for the Perfect Butt," a plain housewife is conditioned to think that she should look like the woman on the cover. By listening to the discreet brags of a visiting aunt about her daughter being the captain of the cheerleading squad, the prom queen, a math whiz, and a valedictorian, a teenager is made to think she should aim to be the same to make her parents proud. By seeing the 35-year old CEO drive his sleek black Jaguar, wear his perfectly fitted tailored suit over his equally perfect physique, play golf and rub elbows with more important men, and date the prettiest models in town, a young employee is influenced to aim for that image of success. These illustrations are examples of visual noises, aural noises, and thought noises.

Staying young and sexy, becoming an achiever, and aiming for success, of course, aren't bad goals. On the contrary, they are ideal. The problem arises, however, when reaching for these goals have started to look bleak, have become entirely unattainable, or despite having been successful, the person fails to find satisfaction from it, because this is when anxiety and depression creeps in.

It may sound rather simplistic and narrow because the human experience is after all diverse. A person could be undergoing depression because of medical reasons, another could be experiencing anxiety attacks because of an impending exam, or that a mother could be overwhelmed by stress simply because of the simultaneous needs of her children, the household, and the husband. No matter how far man has gone, however, past realizations remain true; the need to satisfy desires is the root of all misery. To understand this point further, a brief history of the beginning of Buddhism shall be discussed.

SUFFERING

Prince Shakyamuni and his Realization

Before he became the Buddha history has come to know, he was known as Prince Shakyamuni. And like every prince in the fairy tales loved by all, the prince lived a privileged life. Despite the comfort and the protection of his palace walls, however, he found his life to be pointless.

Venturing out of the palace, he discovered that worldly happiness and comfort cannot rid man of his sufferings: old age, illness, and death. To live, therefore, means to be miserable, and he wished to free himself of this misery. Prince Shakyamuni thus left his palace and sought wisdom.

Man's Misery According to Buddha

Realizing the miseries of man is the most important step in every attempt for self-help. This is, after all, where Prince Shakyamuni started his journey in becoming the Buddha. And this is also the first truth he imparts to his followers.

It is thus necessary for the reader to realize the source of his misery. Prince Shakyamuni found the root to be old age, illness and death. Every human being is aware of his or her frailty, and it's this awareness that leads to desire. A person may not be conscious of it, but at the back of his head, there is this need to maximize whatever time he has on this world, or vitality he is granted. He therefore engages in activities where he feels pleasure or those where he experiences satisfaction.

These activities can be virtuous in nature, like a hobby or a profession. And in unfortunate cases, these can be unvirtuous ones such as lust and various addictions.

The problem with satisfaction or pleasure is that the feeling is temporary. Man will eventually seek the same feeling from the same acts. However, the level of pleasure he will feel from his subsequent equal pursuits will never match the pleasure he felt from the first. Therefore, he will seek new activities or engage in more extreme forms of the same acts, otherwise everything becomes monotonous.

Illustration:

Imagine puffing smoke for the first time, and the feeling of satisfaction or relief that followed. The body will survive without a cigarette, but the mind craves for it. As a result, the person will satisfy this craving by indulging once more in a stick. A stick will become two, and two will become three, and eventually, if left uncontrolled, it will rise to a pack or more.

Now imagine having been dependent on cigarettes for years. Everyday after work, you relax by grabbing a cup of coffee while smoking a stick or two. And now think how it would feel if the cigarette is removed from the daily habit. In the very least, it will be agitating, and at most, it will be miserable.

No matter how shallow your attachment is with cigarettes, its absence shall result in misery and thus, in suffering.

It may thus be concluded that by attaching one's desires to material things or worldly pleasures, a person shall never know inner peace because in the crevices of his consciousness, he craves and desires.

Suffering in Noble Pursuits

It is easy to understand how unvirtuous acts such as alcoholism, smoking, sexual indulgence, and substance abuse needs leads to misery. You may now be wondering why acts which aren't necessarily unvirtuous such as hobbies or professions become sources of suffering.

Whether an act is driven by the need to experience pleasure or to practice a passion, as long as there is attachment, suffering shall take root.

Illustration

The movie entitled The Black Swan is perhaps the most apt example. Ballet was the profession and sole passion of the protagonist. Threatened by an equally talented ballerina for the most ambitious role of her career, she sought perfection in her art. The pressure she imposed on herself and the deep envy she harbored caused her peace and her security in the profession to crumble.

Although at the end she still got the role and she had managed to perform the part exquisitely, she was never the same person. The protagonist had forever remained troubled.

On a more relatable example, look at the successful lives of Kate Spade and Anthony Bourdain. In the eyes of the public, they have everything desirable: soaring careers, money, a network of the coolest friends, and millions of followers around the globe. They are adored by everyone, and they have never been the subject of intrigue and examples of moral depravity. And yet they still took their own lives.

At some point in their lives, they dreamed and desired. And through hard work, they achieved. This simple fact should have been enough to bring them pleasure, and perhaps it did. They perhaps came to a realization that despite everything they felt empty.

Of course, the real reason behind Kate Spade and Anthony Bourdain's suicide must have been far more complex than that. Just the same, however, no matter how virtuous your pursuits are, as long as you attach your desires to worldly pleasures, true happiness will only remain just an idea.

Noises as Roots of Suffering

Visual and aural noises, despite being nothing but background hubbub, greatly influence the decisions of an individual. So great that they sometimes dictate what dreams a person should go after.

By being bombarded by thousands of advertisements every day, your mind develops a set of life standards. These standards must then be met, and so you enumerate a series of material desires to support it. This could be the desire to find a job under a specific salary grade, desire to acquire certain objects like an apartment in the heart of New York City, or desire to find true love in the figure of a slim, medium-height brunette with a college degree.

These visual noises are then amplified by aural noises. People hear from parents, bosses, or loved ones what are expected of them. The person's natural reaction to these expectations could be 1) to work hard to meet it, or 2) to strive to not.

People afterwards attach themselves to these desires and expectations and shape their lives according to them.

Meditation will help you silence thought noises, but as explained earlier, these thoughts will rise back in the presence of visual and aural noises. And unfortunately, these two cannot be silenced because they are beyond your control.

What is the point of all this?

No matter how much time you dedicate in meditation, if the objects you familiarize yourself with do not play a material matter in causing anxiety and depression, these two shall continue to thrive. Their presence may not be felt most of the time, but they are there, suppressed by the temporary alleviation of stress.

And this is why this book has included this chapter.

It serves as a guide on what specific aspect of your life you should focus on to alleviate anxiety and depression.

What object do you need to meditate on, therefore, to pinpoint the root of anxiety and depression?

As you may have already gleaned from previous discussions, the answer is attachments and expectations. The former however takes different forms, and it is up to you to know which form yours took. And because this can be virtuous acts, finding them just made it more difficult.

There may even be instances where these attachments are layered under a series of unvirtuous, but nonetheless immaterial, acts. All this time you could be meditating on the little vices you've been keeping, and still wonder why the anxiety and depression still haunts you.

Whatever the case may be, it may take years of

searching before one could find his ultimate attachment. Sometimes even, the person has to lose everything else first to see what this is.

What is the goal of this chapter?

The goal of this chapter is to lead your meditations to the root of suffering. Its purpose is to open your mind to a different perspective.

Every person owns their dreams, purpose and whatever else they thought they imposed upon themselves. And when some start realizing this dream, or when they start living it, the happiness they expected to find from it could not meet their expectations. This leaves them wondering why or where they went wrong. They continue doing what they do, however. The problem is that they cannot find joy in them anymore or at the very least, a sense of purpose. All they could feel from it is stress, anxiety and depression.

When this someone seeks the aid of meditation;

when they seek to help themselves, most book would only provide the process. They will enumerate the how-tos as what was done in the first few chapters, but almost never guide the person spiritually.

Is this chapter applicable to everyone?

People experience life uniquely, and each react to a given situation in life differently. The assumption this creates, therefore, is that this chapter is not applicable to everyone.

You may elect to skip this chapter altogether if you don't find it necessary to your practice. But do keep it. In times of great distress, and when you cannot find the source of this distress, reread this chapter. The simple wisdom it imparts might just help you.

Exercise 4

To help you find your attachment, you only need to answer a single question:

"What is that thing in my life that will make me feel empty when I lose or fail at it?"

Be careful in answering, however. More often than not, people mistake a different thing for their attachment. They only realize which is which when it's gone and they already feel lost or empty.

Another thing you should remember here is that your attachment isn't always tangible, like your career or your family. It can be something abstract and deeper than that like narcissism or the feeling of being needed. There can be cases where you feel that if you lose this very specific job in this very specific company you'd be nothing because it has been your lifelong dream. And say you did lose it, but it didn't make you feel that bad. That's because it's not actually the job that keeps you going, but the glorification you get from it.

Chapter 6: Benefits of Meditation

Relaxation as the Key to a Healthier Body and Mind

The topics under this chapter can be divided into two: one explaining the benefits of meditation on the body, and the other explaining its benefits on the mind and how it alleviates stress, anxiety and depression. It is impractical, however, to do because these two seemingly polar aspects are interrelated.

The general effect of meditation is relaxation. All the worries that bother the mind are dropped for 5 minutes. Despite such a meager number, its effect could transcend throughout the day. And you'd be surprised how much a relaxed body can do to your health.

Breathing

The body gets supplied with plenty of oxygen during meditation despite not being engaged in taxing physical activities.

A person suffering from anemia is burdened with the feeling of exhaustion even if they did nothing physically or mentally draining. The culprit behind this is their low hemoglobin count. Hemoglobin carries oxygen and delivers them to the different parts of the body. Oxygen, in turn, is like the fire that burns fuel to make a machine run. It burns stored sugars and fatty acids, breaks them down and converts them to energy.

Now imagine if not enough oxygen is being delivered throughout the body because of low hemoglobin count. Because there isn't much fire to burn the fuel, the person ends up with less energy. And by having less energy, the person cannot do more with vigor but only the usual everyday tasks.

The same physiological process applies when a

normal person engages in exercise. Because the body needs that extra boost of energy, his body quickens the heart to distribute oxygen faster, and of course, increases the intake of oxygen by breathing faster.

This time, think of how having a surplus of oxygen in the body would affect you in the absence of anemia and exercise. You will feel energized. Just the mere feeling of being energized relieves stress. And having this nuisance off your back, you will feel refreshed and happy.

Having an overall happy disposition relaxes the entire body, and when the body is relaxed, the mind can easily free itself of worry too. This is why breathing is key in meditation.

Another benefit of having ample supplies of oxygen is a clearer mind. Scientists have recommended furnishing rooms with plants to help you focus better on studying or reading. This means that your level of alertness and focus increases by simply being supplied with ample oxygen.

Heart and Immunity

Almost as good as physical exercise in improving heart health, meditation regulates the person's heart rate. Supported by a 2012 study published in the journal *Circulation: Cardiovascular Quality and Outcomes*, meditation reduces risk of high blood pressure, and other cardiovascular related illnesses and events such as stroke, heart attack, and of course, death.

Studies have also shown that meditation drastically decreases risks of illness and infection. The study involves a group of volunteers who practice meditation regularly over eight weeks and another group who don't. After having been given flu shots, their blood was tested and the results have shown that the group of practitioners produced more antibodies against the flu virus.

Mood and Overall Mental Disposition

Another study has proven that meditation can improve mood. With stress, anxiety and depression out of the picture, there's no reason why your mood shouldn't lighten up.

Doctors scanned the brain activity of monks and it has shown that their brains are significantly active in areas associated with happiness and learning than people who do not practice meditation. Another interesting result of this study is the finding of evidence that there is improved conscious perception, memory and attention.

Furthermore, because the practice disciplines you on controlling reactions, viewing thoughts without judgment, and being critical on certain aspects of life, you learn to let go of negative thoughts and emotions.

These benefits and effects are not brought solely by mental discipline, but also by the breathing exercise. If you think about it, the entire practice produces a chain of results. One good thing influencing another good thing to bring about a holistically positive outcome.

Beginners must know, however, that these physical and mental benefits will not reflect overnight. The studies that proved these results observed people who have been practicing meditation for over 10 years.

Neither can beginners rush the effects of meditation. This is a long process, one that will take years. When compared to medicine, it may seem that meditation is not a practical solution at all. Understand, however, that the practice comes at minimal cost and no side effects.

EXTENDED BENEFITS OF ZAZEN AND QI GONG EXERCISES

The strict application of form and posture in Zazen is not without purpose. Although the person does not undergo intensive physical exercise; that instead they remain still, they still reap permanent physical benefits.

Better Posture

Because of bad habits and being unconscious of it, most people are doomed to suffer from chronic back pains later on in their life. Sitting eight hours straight in front of the computer, for example, without minding their posture, causes some parts of the spine to curve unnaturally. Another example would be spending significant amounts of time bending the neck to look at your phone. This causes the upper portion of the spine to take the entire weight of the head.

Zen meditation corrects the form of the neck and spine by re-aligning them. This thus prevents the permanence of unnatural curvatures caused by improper postures.

Improved Flexibility

Bending your legs and keeping them bent even for just five minutes isn't easy. If the muscles are tight, this would be next to impossible. And should you be able to maintain this posture, you'd end up with cramped legs.

If you do the simple exercises recommended earlier, however, your flexibility would greatly improve. And this will allow you to not only bend your legs, but also teach you to bend from the knees and not from your hips.

The danger of bending from the hips is that it's unnatural, and will later on cause back pains more especially if the spine is curved in the process. This is extra dangerous if the reason you're bending is because you need to pick something heavy. Improved flexibility in your legs, however, will make it easier for the knees to bend and allow the legs to carry all the weight of the upper body and the item to picked up.

Blood Pressure Relief

This is the direct benefit of the Qi Gong exercise Painting with Light. The movements distribute and moderate the flow of blood to and from certain points of your body.

Relief from Asthma

The Qi Gong movement called Opening the Energy Gates comes with this specific benefit. Because the arms are pulled wide open, the lungs are stretched and thus revitalized. It allows the organ to expand and open for a better intake of air.

Chapter 7: Frequently Asked Questions

I have been meditating religiously for quite some time now. But I cannot feel it take effect. Am I doing something wrong?

This book can only help in a broad and general manner. Meditation is a highly personal process. And in reality, what goes on inside you, apart from being unique, cannot be fully expressed in words. If you come to this situation, the best solution is to find a master, attend his classes, and seek his guidance. The wisdom he is capable of imparting is beyond measure and one that cannot be contained in a book.

What time of the day is best for the practice?

As mentioned in the earlier chapters, meditating immediately after waking up is best. As to exactly what time you should wake up, the answer would be four in the morning. The world is still asleep, you are alone and your mind is highly active.

Claims of better brain productivity at this time remains a subject of debates. It cannot be denied, however, that countless notable personalities such as Tim Cook, Anna Wintour and Michelle Obama start their day from between 3:45 am and 5:00 am. The following are the benefits of a 4:00 am waking time:

- Every minute from the time you wake up until about seven in the morning is exclusively yours. Expect no one to bother you around these hours, except only for children if you have any.

- You cannot bother anyone at these hours. Most people are still asleep, and if there are important matters at work, these would have to wait. You therefore have no other choice but to spend your minutes for other things -- meditation perhaps.

☐ If you get full hours of sleep, your brain is fully awake and ready to function. Maximize this activity for your personal benefit instead of answering emails.

Meditating at four in the morning, however, will not be effective if you do not fill in your required hours of sleep. You must, therefore, adjust your bedtime to nine or ten in the evening. If that's not possible, then don't force the 4:00 am call time.

I want to listen to music during meditation. What specific type of genre is best?

It has been mentioned earlier that you can supplement analytical meditations with instrumental music. As for the genre, Indian classical music at 432 Hz is the tune to go for. The tune creates a positive shift in your energy by silencing thoughts of worry, and thus helping your mind focus on meditation. The recommended frequency, on the other hand, promotes healing. According to scientists, 432 Hz is the frequency of the universe. Music tuned to this pitch therefore is softer for the ears and thus more relaxing.

How will I know if I'm making progress in meditation?

When you think you're more at peace than before, then your practice is working. Some indicators of being at peace are your conduct, your senses and your reactions. If you feel that you've become a little calmer, and that you don't hurry from one task to another anymore, there is progress. If your eyes, for example, can remain steady in a place filled with stimulus, and yet you are still aware of your surroundings, there is progress. If your reaction to traffic is understanding and not pure anger; that you understand that everyone stuck in it is just trying to get from one place to another like you, there is progress.

Is it possible for a person to meditated too much?

Anything in excess is bad for you. Monks can stay in meditation for days, but their objective is different from yours. It is their way of life because they seek enlightenment. You, on the other hand, simply practice meditation to relieve stress, anxiety and depression. Therefore, it is recommended that you peg your practice at a maximum of twenty to twenty-five minutes.

Five to six minutes was recommended in the earlier chapters to ease beginners into the practice. You may, however, opt to spend less or more time on meditation. Just make sure your discretion isn't derived from pure logic. You must listen to your body as well.

In sleep, the body dictates the right time for the mind to wake. Even without an alarm clock, a person will naturally rise from sleep. If for example the person decides to be awakened before his body's dictation or to go back to sleep after his body has just woke him up, he will feel tired even if he had just risen.

The same is true for meditation. The body will dictate the perfect time to rise from the practice. Force meditation and you may do more harm to yourself spiritually.

I might fall asleep while meditating. If that happens, would it mean I am doing something wrong? Is this a common problem?

Falling asleep while meditating isn't exactly common, but it does happen, and it could be due to different reasons. Evaluate yourself and see if any of the following circumstances are applicable in your case:

- You didn't get enough sleep for the day. In the hierarchy of needs, sleep and ample rest would first have to be satisfied before the mind can engage in any other activity, especially one as boring as meditation. If therefore you simply lack sleep, take a nap if you can afford it, then engage in meditation after.

- You've been meditating beyond your usual period. As has just been discussed, the body will dictate the perfect time to rise from the practice. If you decide to push forward, one of the possible effects is falling asleep. When this happens, stop and end your meditation.

- <u>You underwent intense physical exercise before the practice.</u> Intense physical exercise exhaust not only the body but also the mind. If you think about it, physical exercise itself is meditation because the mind is clear of worries and problems, and is instead focused on attaining the goal—running for 10 kilometers, for example. In this circumstance, rest first before engaging in meditation. If you exercise in the morning, consider practicing in the evening before going to bed.

- <u>You had just eaten a large meal</u>. The reason why siestas are best taken after a hefty lunch is because the body places all its effort in digesting the food. Also, it's every human being's survival instinct to become lazy after a large meal. The body can afford to mute the senses because there's currently no need to stay alert to hunt for prey. Like with exercise, the solution here is to let the body take its well-deserved nap and meditate later in the day.

If, however, your only available time of the day for meditation is right after breakfast, lunch, or dinner, then it's best to moderate your food intake instead. Eat just enough to satisfy the grumblings of an empty stomach, but not too much to satisfy gluttony.

- You were lying down during meditation and not in any position that prompts the body to stay alert and awake. If this happens, then sit up straight or better yet, assume one of the positions enumerated in Zazen.

- You feel like your mind is trying to run away from something in meditation. It is possible to doze off during meditation even if none of the abovementioned has occurred. This is especially true for those with busy minds. Compared to an internet browser, these people constantly have 20 tabs open and running simultaneously.

In meditation, the goal is to close all these tabs. And because the mind is somewhat forced to do nothing, it takes the opportunity to shut down and rest.

There is no other solution here but to return to meditation after catching yourself fall asleep. This is how the mind works and you can only train it through sheer willpower.

What do I do when something itches during meditation?

You endure it. Meditation teaches the human mind to choose to not react. Remember that in meditation, when thoughts with associated feelings arrive, you let it pass without judgement. The same discipline should be harbored physically. As a practitioner, you should realize that what you choose to do is different from what you perceive, and what you think or feel. You must realize that all reactions are not automatic – you have a choice.

Should I postpone meditation sessions when I have runny nose?

Same with enduring an

itch, resist the body's automatic response to a runny nose. Instead, observe the feeling.

However, if you have flu and letting your nose run would just make a distracting mess, wipe your nose in the most mindful manner. Accomplish the task with minimal movement. And for this purpose, keep tissues nearby during meditation.

This book keeps on saying to do things naturally. Being conscious of every single thing I do, however, makes me controlling instead. Am I missing something?

This is normal for beginners. Everything will feel awkward as you're still trying to find balance between being relaxed and being aware. At first, you will try to adjust and control. When you notice you're doing this unintentionally, however, stop and let your body be. Your mind and body will soon reach harmony.

Is it alright to practice meditation concurrently with physical exercise? Which should I do first in the morning?

Meditation and physical exercise is the perfect duo. Both the mind and body need equal effort to be disciplined to acquire the benefits of meditation faster and holistically.

As to which to do first in the morning, the answer would depend on the intensity of your exercise. If it makes you tired, then meditate first so you won't have to fall asleep while practicing. If, however, you only do light exercises like yoga or the Qi Gong moves enumerated in the earlier Chapter, it is recommended that you meditate after.

Light exercises quicken the heartbeat and hasten the breathing. These physiological responses awaken the mind and body but not drain you of energy. With the mind alert, you are unlikely to fall asleep during meditation.

Allow the body to rest, however, before moving on to meditation. Let your heart rate calm down and your breathing to slow down. Remember that the body should be in a calm disposition, or in a meditative state, before beginning the practice.

I have a very strict work and personal schedule. Is it possible to practice meditation in the office?

Instead of opting for a solid 15 minutes to practice meditation, try chopping this to 2 minutes every two hours. As you sit in front of the computer, waiting for an email or a large file to finish downloading. take the opportunity to slip into meditation. No one would even notice that you've stopped for two minutes. If, on the other hand, you're not stuck inside the office and is in fact in several different places in a day, try meditating for 3 minutes before every meal. Drop your phone as you wait for your order if you're in a restaurant. Or sink into a prayer-like trance before starting to eat.

Don't worry about the results because whether you do solid or partial meditation, the benefits you will garner will be the same. It is recommended, however, that you do partial meditation only when you already have a good grip on your mind. Because if you don't, you would only end up spending the two minutes trying to silence settle down your worries and problems. If you can enter the meditative state at the snap of a finger, that's when you may go for partial meditation.

Conclusion:

As a parting reminder in meditation and in the truths that you will unearth later on, keeping an open heart is prime. The truth hurts sometimes and it could be something that runs contrary to your well-established beliefs. It will cause you to feel many unpleasant things, but for it to change you for the better, you must keep an open heart. Everything else will follow.

Another parting message is to stay patient. As mentioned earlier, the results of meditation will not manifest overnight. Like with all other things in your adult life, wishing it without working for it will result to nothing. Therefore, if you truly wish to be better, be religious in the practice of meditation. Do it every day and be sincere in the practice.

Again, meditation can help you achieve your

objective of relieving stress, anxiety and depression. Once you see improvements, however, don't stop. Meditation is not a temporary solution. It seeks to discipline the mind and help you live a life free of negative perceptions and emotions.

You will discover a lot of things about yourself through this never-ending journey. And you will be surprised as to how much it can change you.

OTHER BOOKS BY SUSAN MORI

Book 1 :

Yoga: for Beginners: Your Natural Way to Strengthen Your Body, Calming Your Mind and Be in The Moment

Book 2 :

Zen for Beginners: Your Guide to Achieving Happiness and Finding Inner Peace with Zen in Your Everyday Life

Book 3 :

Chakras for Beginners: a Practical Guide to Heal and Balance Yourself through the Power of Chakras

DID YOU ENJOY THIS BOOK?

I want to thank you for purchasing and reading this book. I really hope you got a lot out of it.

Can I ask a quick favor though?

If you enjoyed this book I would really appreciate it if you could leave me a positive review on Amazon.

I love getting feedback from my customers and reviews on Amazon really do make a difference. I read all my reviews and would really appreciate your thoughts.

Thanks so much.

Susan Mori

p.s. You can click here to go directly to the book on Amazon and leave your review.

83769117R00071

Made in the USA
Middletown, DE
14 August 2018